Coaches

BY CECILIA MINDEN

The
**Child's
World**

Published by The Child's World®
1980 Lookout Drive • Mankato, MN 56003-1705
800-599-READ • www.childsworld.com

Acknowledgments
The Child's World®: Mary Berendes, Publishing Director
The Design Lab: Design
Jody Jensen Shaffer: Editing

Photos
Aspen Photo/Shutterstock.com: 10-11, 16;
bikeriderlondon/Shutterstock.com: 12; BrandX:
cover, 1; Cecilia Minden: 9; Fotokostic/Shutterstock.
com: 8; Kim Abrams: 18; Monkey Business Images/
Shutterstock.com: 6-7; Nejc Vesel/Shutterstock.
com: 5; PhotoDisc: design elements; Pressmaster/
Shutterstock.com: 22; Studio 1One/Shutterstock.com:
4; Wallenrock/Shutterstock.com: 20-21

ISBN 9781626870109
LCCN 2013947289

Printed in the United States of America
Mankato, MN
December, 2013
PA02191

ABOUT THE AUTHOR

Dr. Cecilia Minden is a university professor and reading specialist with classroom and administrative experience in grades K–12. She is the author of many books for early readers. Cecilia and her husband, Dave Cupp, live in North Carolina. She earned her PhD in reading education from the University of Virginia.

CONTENTS

Hello, My Name Is Jack.

Many people live and work in my neighborhood. Each of them helps the neighborhood in different ways.

I thought of all the things I like to do. I like to eat healthy foods and get plenty of exercise. I like to play sports with my friends. I like to help others learn new things. How could I help my neighborhood when I grow up?

If you like sports, maybe one day it could be your job.

I Could Be a Coach!

Coaches like to play sports. They know that teamwork and good health are very important.

Best of all, coaches get to help other people become better players!

A good coach should enjoy helping others.

Learn About This Neighborhood Helper!

The best way to learn is to ask questions. Words such as *who*, *what*, *where*, *when*, and *why* will help me learn about being a coach.

Asking a coach questions will help you learn more about the job.

Who Can Become a Coach?

Boys and girls who like sports may want to become coaches. People who want to be coaches must also enjoy helping others learn new skills. There are many different kinds of sports, so there are many different kinds of coaches.

Coaches are important neighborhood helpers. They give people a chance to get involved in healthy, fun activities. They also teach important skills such as listening, following directions, and working together.

Coaches teach players important skills, including teamwork.

Meet a Coach!

This is Coach Susan Crammar. She coaches girls' lacrosse in Chapel Hill, North Carolina. Lacrosse is a ball game played outdoors with two

How Many Coaches Are There?
About 130,000 people work as coaches. Another 180,000 volunteer as coaches.

Coach Crammar helps players improve their lacrosse skills.

teams. Each team has long sticks with small nets on the end. Players use the nets to pass the ball and to score goals on the field.

Coach Crammar played many sports when she was a young girl. When she is not coaching, she likes to spend time with her family. Her two daughters also like to play sports.

Lacrosse takes a lot of teamwork, especially to score a goal!

Where Can I Learn to Be a Coach?

Coach Crammar went to college to become a coach. She learned how to coach many different kinds of sports, including swimming, diving, and gymnastics.

There are also volunteer coaches. These coaches offer to work with players for no pay. Volunteer coaches may not get paid, but they still need to know a lot about a certain sport. They must train players to have the skills that will help them win!

How Much School Will I Need?
Most high school, college, and professional coaches have a four-year college degree. Coaches in public schools must pass a test given by the sate where they live. They are then given a license so they can work.

Coaches must know a lot about their sport.

What Does a Coach Need to Do the Job?

Coach Crammar uses a rule book, a whistle, and a stop watch. Coaches sometimes carry a clipboard with paper for drawing plays. This helps the team see what they are supposed to do on the field.

Coaches need to make sure that their team has the right equipment for the sport they are playing. Coach Crammar's lacrosse team needs goal

What Are Some Tools I Will Use?
- Exercise and training equipment
- Various sports equipment
- Video cameras
- White board and markers

nets, balls, sticks, and special gear to protect their eyes and mouths.

Coach Crammar also uses special words to talk about lacrosse with her team. Lacrosse players learn to cradle the ball. This means they learn how to keep the ball in the basket part of their stick. They also learn how to **shoot** the ball past the goalie and into the **cage** to score. The goalie's job is to keep the other team's ball from going into the cage.

Many coaches do their work in a gymnasium.

Where Does a Coach Work?

Coach Crammar teaches at a high school. She comes to work early in the morning and helps the other coaches set up the gym for **physical education** (PE) classes. Coach Crammar and the other coaches set up nets, hurdles, and balls in the gym. Her students might also watch videos, read books, have talks about keeping healthy, and take tests.

What's It Like Where I'll Work?
Coaches work both indoors and outdoors. They often work inside gymnasiums and stadiums. Coaches also work on outdoor fields. Sometimes it is very hot or very cold outside. It might snow or rain during practice or games.

How Much Money Will I Make?

Most coaches make between $18,000 and $45,000 a year. Professional coaches can make much more.

Coach Crammar works with her girls' lacrosse team on the field after school. She usually spends a lot time the night before deciding what skills and plays her team will practice the next day.

Coaches spend part of the day on the field with their team.

Who Works with Coaches?

Many people help Coach Crammar do her job. Other coaches help her work with students during PE classes. Parents may help out during lacrosse games. It takes teamwork for all these people to work together, but teamwork is what coaches do best!

Some people coach professional teams. These teams earn money to play sports. Coaches who train professional teams work with managers who are in charge of team business. They also work with doctors who look after injured players.

What other Jobs Might I Like?
- Athletic trainer
- Professional athlete
- Teacher
- Umpire or referee

Coaches often work with referees and umpires.

Kim often attends lacrosse tournaments and sometimes gets to meet professional players.

When is Your Coach Your Mom?

Kim Abrams is a member of the Tuscarora Nation (Turtle Clan) and grew up on the Tuscarora Indian Reservation in upstate New York. She is also the proud mother of three lacrosse players. Kim coaches her daughter on the International First Nations Women's lacrosse team. Kim teaches forth grade at Tuscarora Indian Elementary School in Lewiston, New York.

How Might My Job Change?
Many high school coaches eventually teach at the college level. Sometimes college coaches are hired by professional sports teams.

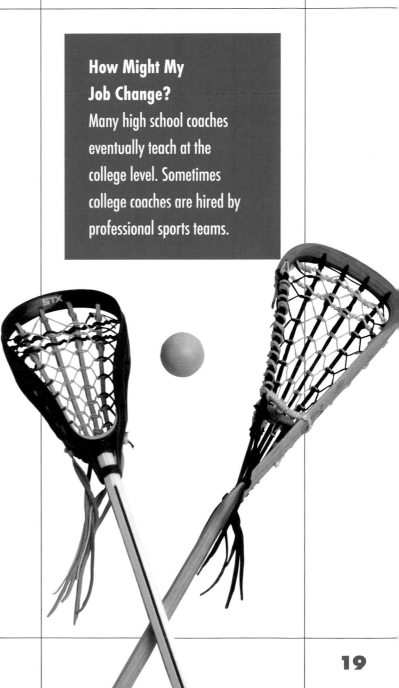

I Want to Be a Coach!

I think being a coach would be a great way to be a neighborhood helper. Someday I may be coaching your favorite team!

Is This Job Growing?
The need for coaches will grow more than other jobs.

Maybe one day you'll help players become better athletes!

Why Don't You Try Being a Coach?

Do you think you would like to be a coach? A coach knows that an important skill in all sports is good **coordination**. You can improve your coordination by jumping rope, playing hopscotch, throwing a ball at a target, or learning to juggle. Practice one or all of these activities as often as you can.

Invite your friends to join in, too. Coordination is a big part of teamwork. Coaches need to bring players together so they can pass a ball, score a goal, or stop the other team from getting a home run. Everyone needs to know how to use the right moves at the right time.

Coaches help all members of a team coordinate.

GLOSSARY

cage (KAYJ) a net or goal box used in sports

coordination (koh-or-duh-NAY-shuhn) keeping your hands, eyes, and feet all moving the right way at the same time

physical education (FIZ-uh-kuhl ej-uh-KAY-shuhn) classes that teach students how to play different sports and do activities that will help them stay in shape

shoot (SHOOT) to aim and launch a ball

LEARN MORE ABOUT COACHES

BOOKS

Finchler, Judy, and Kevin O'Malley (illustrator). *You're a Good Sport, Miss Malarkey.* New York: Walker & Co., 2004.

Nelson, Robin. *Coaches.* Minneapolis, MN: Lerner Publications, 2005.

WEB SITES

Visit our home page for lots of links about coaches:

www.childsworld.com/links

Note to Parents, Teachers, and Librarians: We routinely check our Web links to make sure they're safe, active sites—so encourage your readers to check them out!

INDEX

8/14